THE WEALTH COMPASS

21 KEYS TO UNLOCKING FINANCIAL SUCCESS

By

Dr. James F. Bass

DISCLAIMER

Table of contents

Contents

DISCLAIMER 1

THE PRINCIPLES FOR PROCURING WEALTH 6

KEY SIX 37

RELY ON YOUR OWN EFFORT 37

UTILIZE THE BEST DEVICE 41

DO NOT GROW ABOVE YOUR 43

BUSINESS 43

KEY NINE 51

LEARN SOMETHING USEFUL 51

KEY TEN 52

LET HOPE PREDOMINATE, BUT BE NOT TOO VISIONARY 52

KEY TWELVE ....BE SYSTEMATIC54

KEY THIRTEEN 55

READ THE PAPERS DAILY......................55

KEY FOURTEEN....................................56

BE CAREFUL WITH OUTDOOR ACTIVITY 56

KEY FIFTEEN...58

TRY NOT TO INDORSE WITHOUT SECURITY...58

KEY SIXTEEN...62

PUBLICIZE YOUR BUSINESS.................62

YOUR CLIENTS......................................66

BE MAGNANIMOUS 68

KEY NINETEEN 70

TRY NOT TO BLAB 70

KEY TWEWNTY 71

PROTECT YOUR HONESTY....................71

KEY   TWENTY ONE.......................... CAREFULLY CHOOSE   AND   MAKE DECISIONS......................................75

INTRODUCTION

In the present always impacting world, making financial progress is by all accounts a tricky dream for some. In any case, "The wealth Compass: 21 Keys unlocking financial success" offers an encouraging sign, directing you towards a prosperous future.

In this book, we dig into the center standards and down to earth systems that will assist you with exploring the maze of wealth creation. Whether you are a beginner financial backer or an accomplished business visionary, this book is intended to act as your confided in sidekick on the excursion towards monetary freedom.

"The wealth Compass" isn't just about collecting cash; it is about developing a mentality that draws in overflow, creating strong monetary plans, and pursuing informed choices to secure and develop your riches. Through its 18 enabling keys, you will acquire the vital devices and information to   open the   ways to monetary achievement.

Each key is unpredictably woven with genuine models, master experiences, and significant advances that can be applied in your own monetary undertakings. From excelling at planning and saving to savvy effective money management, from understanding the influence of recurring, automated revenue to bridling the capability of business venture, this book covers a large number of subjects that are fundamental for building a strong financial establishment.

"The wealth Compass" isn't simply a guide to independence from the rat race; an extraordinary aid enables you to change your monetary predetermination. It adjusts your compass and focuses you in the correct course, empowering you to explore the exciting bends in the road of the monetary world with certainty and clearness.

Prepare to leave on a groundbreaking excursion that will assist you with opening your full monetary potential. Let "The wealth Compass" be your directing light towards a fate of financial success, harmony, and overflow.

THE PRINCIPLES FOR PROCURING WEALTH

In the US where there is more land than individuals, it isn't the slightest bit hard for people healthy to bring in cash. In this similarly new field there are such countless roads of achievement open, such countless occupations which are not swarmed, that any individual of either sex who is willing, until further notice, to take part in any decent occupation that offers, may view as rewarding work.

The individuals who truly want to achieve freedom, have just to set their minds upon it, and take on the legitimate means, as they in all actuality do with respect to some other object which they wish to achieve, and the thing is effortlessly finished. In any case, even though it could be found to bring in cash, I have no question that a significant number of my listeners will concur it is the most troublesome thing on the planet to keep. The way to abundance is, as plain as the way to the factory." It comprises basically in exhausting short of what we procure; that is by all accounts an exceptionally straightforward issue.

One of those cheerful manifestations of the friendly Dickens, places the case in a solid light when he expresses that to have yearly pay of twenty pounds for every annum, and burn through twenty pounds and sixpence, is to be the most hopeless of men; though, to have a pay of just twenty pounds, and spend however nineteen pounds and sixpence is to be the most joyful of humans. A significant number of my followers may say, we grasp this: this is an economy, and we realize the economy is abundant; we realize we can't eat our cake and keep it likewise. Yet maybe more instances of disappointment emerge from blotches on this point than practically some other. The truth of the matter is, numerous Individuals think they comprehend the economy when they truly don't. Genuine economy is misunderstood, and individuals carry on with existence without appropriately fathoming what that guideline is. According to one, "I have a pay of so much, and here is my neighbor who has something very similar; yet consistently he gets something ahead and I miss the mark; for what reason is it? I have a ton of familiarity with financial matters. He figures he does, however he doesn't. There are men who imagine that economy consists in saving cheddar pairings and light closures, in removing two pence from the laundress' bill and doing a wide range of pretty much nothing, mean, filthy things. Economy isn't ugliness.

The disaster is, additionally, that this class of people let their economy apply in just a single bearing. They are extravagant, they are so magnificently affordable in saving a half-penny where they should burn through two pence that they want to bear to waste this way and that. Before lamp fuel oil was found or considered, one could stop for the time being at practically any rancher's home in the horticultural locale and get an excellent dinner, however after dinner he could endeavor to peruse in the parlor, and would track down it unimaginable with the wasteful light of one flame. The entertainer, seeing his problem, would agree: "It is fairly hard to peruse here nights; the adage says 'you should have a boat adrift to have the option to consume two candles at once; we never have an additional light besides additional events." These extra events happen, maybe, two times every year. In this manner the great lady saves five, six, or ten bucks in that time: yet the data which may be gotten from having the additional light would, obviously, far offset a lot of candles. In any case, the difficulty doesn't end here. It is so practical to feel that she in fat confections, she wants to bear to go often to the town and burn through twenty or thirty bucks for strips and furbelows, a considerable lot of which are not fundamental. This bogus simply could habitually be found in men of business, and in those cases it frequently hurries to composing paper. You track down great finance managers who save every one of the old envelopes and scraps, and wouldn't tear another piece of paper, if they could stay away from it, for the world. This is all well overall; they may in this way save five or ten bucks per year, yet being so prudent just in note paper, they think they can stand to sit around idly; to host costly get-togethers, and to drive their carriages. This is an outline saving at the nozzle and squandering at the bung opening not great with finances. Punch in talking of this one thought class of individuals says they resemble the one who purchased a penny herring for his family's supper and afterward employed a mentor and four to bring it back home.

I never knew a man to prevail by rehearsing this sort of economy. Genuine economy continuously causes the pay to surpass the outgo, wear the old garments somewhat longer if vital; shed the new sets of gloves; patch the old dress: live on planer food assuming need be; so that, under all conditions, except if some unanticipated mishap happens, there will be an edge in favor of the pay. A penny here, and a dollar there, put at revenue, continues aggregating, and in this way the ideal outcome is achieved. It requires some preparing, maybe, to achieve this economy, however when accustomed to it, you will find there is more fulfillment in sane saving than in silly spending.

Here is a recipe which I suggest: I have tracked down it to work a superb solution for excess, and particularly for a mixed economy.

At the point when you find that you have no excess toward the year's end, but have a great pay, I encourage you to take a couple of pieces of paper and structure them into a book and discount each thing of consumption. Post it consistently or weekly in two segments, one headed necessaries or even solaces, and the other headed extravagances, and you will find that the last segment will be twofold, high pitch, and as often as possible multiple times more prominent than the previous. The genuine solaces of life cost however a little piece of what a large portion of us can procure. It is the eyes of others and not our own eyes which ruin us. On the off chance that all the world were visually impaired aside from myself i shouldn't care for fine garments or furniture. In America numerous people like to rehash we are free and rise to, however it is an extraordinary slip-up in additional faculties than one.

That we are conceived "free and rise to" is a magnificent truth in one sense, yet we are not all conceived similarly rich, and we never will be.

One might say; there is a man who has a pay of 50,000 bucks per annum, while I have however 1,000 bucks; I knew that individual when he was unfortunate such as myself; presently he is rich and thinks he is superior to I'm; I will show him that I am on par with what he is; I will proceed to purchase a pony and buggy; no, I can't do that, yet I will proceed to enlist one and ride this midday on the equivalent street that he does, and accordingly demonstrate to him that I am on par with what he is.

My companion, you really want not to take that difficulty; you can without much of a stretch demonstrate that you are on par with what he is; you have just to act as well as he does; however you can't cause anyone to accept that you are rich as he is. Moreover, assuming you put on these airs, add burn through your time and spend your cash, your unfortunate spouse will be obliged to clean her fingers off at home, and get her tea two ounces all at once, and all the other things in extent, all together that you might keep up appearances, and, all things considered, misdirect no one. Then again, Mrs. Smith might say that her next door neighbor wedded Johnson for his cash, and "everyone says as much." She has a pleasant 1,000 dollar camel's hair wrap, and she will cause Smith to get her an impersonation one, and she will sit in a seat right close to her neighbor in the chapel, in request to demonstrate that she is her equivalent.

My great lady, you won't excel on the planet, if your vanity and envy accordingly starts to lead the pack. In this nation, where we accept the larger part should rule, we overlook that standard concerning design, and let a modest bunch of individuals, calling themselves the privileged, run up a misleading norm of flawlessness, and in attempting to ascend to that norm, we continually keep ourselves poor; all the time searching away for outside appearances. How much more shrewd to be a regulation no matter what anyone else might think" and say, we will control our out go by our pay, and lay up something for a blustery day. Individuals should be as reasonable regarding the matter of cash getting as on some other subject. Like causes produced like outcomes. You can't gather a fortune by taking the street that prompts destitution. It needs no prophet to let us know that the individuals who live completely up to their means, with no thought of an opposite in this life, can never achieve monetary freedom. People familiar with satisfy each impulse and eccentricity, will track down it hard, from the start, to chop down their different pointless costs, and will feel it an extraordinary discipline to reside in a more modest house than they have been familiar with more affordable furnishings, less organization, less expensive dress, less workers, a less number of balls, parties, theater-goings, carriage-ridings, delight journeys, stogie smoking, alcohol drinking, and different luxuries; in any case, late all, in the event that they will attempt the arrangement of laying by a "savings," or, as such, a little amount of cash, at premium or wisely put resources into land, they will be astonished at the joy to be gotten from continually adding to their little heap, as well as from every one of the practical propensities which are caused by this course. The old suit of garments, and the old cap and dress, will deal with another season; the Croton or spring water taste better compared to champagne; a virus shower and an energetic walk will demonstrate more thrilling than a ride in the best mentor; a social talk, a night's perusing in the family circle, or an hour's play of chase the shoe" and visually impaired man's buff" will be definitely more lovely than a fifty or five hundred dollar party, when the reflection on the distinction in cost is enjoyed by the people who start to know the joys of saving. Large number of men are kept poor, and several thousands are made so after they have gained very adequate to help them well through life, in the outcome of laying their arrangements of living on too expansive a stage. A few families use as much as 20,000 dollars per annum, and some substantially more, and would barely know how to live on less, while others secure more strong pleasure habitually on a 20th part of that sum. Thriving is a more serious trial than misfortune, particularly unexpected success.

"What was easy to get is just as easy to lose," is an old and genuine adage. A feeling of pride and vanity, when allowed to have full influence, is the undying blister worm which chews the actual vitals of a man's common belongings, let them be little or incredible, hundreds, or millions. Numerous people, as they thrive, promptly grow their thoughts and begin consuming extravagances, until in a brief time frame their costs gobble up their pay, and they become destroyed in their ludicrous endeavors to keep up appearances, and make a sensation. According to a man of his word of fortune who, when he initially started to thrive, his spouse would have a new and rich couch. That couch, he says, cost me thirty thousand bucks! When the couch arrived at the house, it was found important to get seats to coordinate; then, at that point, side-sheets, covers and tables to compare with them, through the whole supply of furniture; when finally it was found that the actual house was excessively little and dated for the furnishings, and a new one was worked to compare with the new buys; consequently, added my companion, summarizing a cost of 30,000 bucks, brought about by that solitary couch, and outfitting on me, looking like workers, hardware, and the vital costs specialist after keeping up a fine 'foundation,' a yearly expense of eleven thousand bucks, and a tight squeeze at that: while, a decade prior, we lived with significantly more genuine solace, on the grounds that with considerably less consideration, on as numerous hundreds. In all actuality," he proceeded, "that couch would have carried me to unavoidable, had not a most unexampled title to flourish, kept me above it, and had I not really looked at the normal longing to 'cut a scramble.

The underpinning of progress in life is great wellbeing: that is the foundation fortune; it is additionally the premise of joy. An individual can't collect a fortune very well when he is debilitated. He has no desire; no impetus; no power. Obviously, there are the people who have awful wellbeing and can't resist: you can't anticipate that such people can collect riches, however there are a large number of in chronic frailty who need not be so. On the off chance that, sound wellbeing is the groundwork of accomplishment and joy throughout everyday life, how significant it is that we ought to concentrate on the laws of wellbeing, which is yet another articulation for the laws of nature! The closer we keep to the laws of nature, the closer we are to great wellbeing, but the number of people there that are who pay no thoughtfulness regarding normal regulations, however totally violate them, even against their own regular tendency. We should know that the transgression of obliviousness is rarely winked at concerning the infringement of nature's regulations; their infraction generally brings the punishment. A kid might push its finger into the blazes without realizing it will consume, thus endures, atonement, even, won't stop the brilliant. A considerable lot of our progenitors had close to zero familiarity with the rule of ventilation. They didn't have any idea much about oxygen, whatever other "gin" they could have been familiar with; what's more, thusly they constructed their homes with minimal seven-by-nine feet rooms, and furthermore, these old fashioned devout Puritans would secure themselves in one of these cells, say their requests and hit the hay. Toward the beginning of the day they would faithfully return gratitude for the "conservation of their lives," during the evening, and no one had better motivation to be grateful. Presumably some enormous break in the window, or in the entryway, let in a little outside air, and consequently saved them.

Numerous people purposely abuse the laws of nature against their better motivations, for style. For example, there is one thing that nothing living with the exception of a disgusting worm at any point normally cherishes, and that is tobacco; yet the number of people there are who purposely train an unnatural hunger, and beat this embedded revolution for tobacco, so much that they get to adore it. They have hold of a toxic, foul weed, or rather that takes a firm hold of them.

Here are hitched men who run about spitting tobacco juice on the floor covering and floors, and once in a while even upon their spouses other than. They don't kick their spouses out of entryways like tipsy men, yet their spouses, I feel somewhat unsure, frequently wish they were beyond the house. Another unsafe component is that this counterfeit craving, like envy, "develops by what it benefits from;" when you love what is unnatural, a more grounded craving is made for the harmful thing than the normal longing for what is innocuous. There is an old axiom which says that "propensity is second nature," however a counterfeit propensity is more grounded than nature. Take for example, an old tobacco-chewer; his affection for the "quid" is more grounded than his adoration for a specific sort of food. He can surrender a broiled hamburger simpler than surrender the weed. Youthful chaps lament that they are not men; they might want to hit the hay young men also, awaken men; and to achieve this they duplicate the vices of their seniors. Little Tommy and Johnny see their dads or uncles smoke a line, and they say, "On the off chance that I could do that, I would take care of business as well; Uncle John has gone out what's more, left his line of tobacco, let us attempt it." They take a match and light it, and afterward puff away. "We will figure out how to smoke; do you like it Johnny?" That fellow drearily answers: "Not without question; it tastes harsh;" before long he develops pale, however he

perseveres parched he before long proposals up a penance on the special raised area of style; yet the young men stick to it also, drive forward until finally they overcome their normal cravings and become the survivors of mixed bags.

Take the tobacco-chewer. Toward the beginning of the day, when he gets up, he puts a quid in his mouth and keeps it there the entire day, never taking it out but to trade it for a new one, or when he will eat; goodness! Indeed, at stretches during the day and evening, numerous a chewer takes out the quid and grasps it sufficiently long to take a beverage, and afterward pop it returns once more. This basically demonstrates that the hunger for rum is much more grounded than that for tobacco. At the point when the tobacco-chewer goes to your nation seat and you show him your grapery and organic product house, and the wonders of your nursery, when you offer him some new, ready organic product, and say, My companion, I have here the most delectable apples, and pears, and peaches, and apricots; I have imported them from Spain, France and Italy simply see those tasty grapes; there isn't anything more delectable nor more sound than ready organic product, so help yourself; I need to see you enchant yourself with these things; he will roll the dear quid under his tongue and reply, "No, I thank you, I have tobacco in my mouth.

His sense of taste has become narcotized by the poisonous weed, and he has lost, in an extraordinary measure, the fragile and lucky preference for organic products. This shows what costly, pointless and damaging propensities men will get into. I talk from experience. I have smoked until I shuddered like an aspen leaf, the blood hurried to my head, and I had a palpitation of the heart which I believed was coronary illness, till I was nearly killed with trepidation. At the point when I counseled my doctor, he said break off tobacco utilizing." I was not just harming my wellbeing and spending a lot of cash, yet I was setting a terrible model. I submitted to his advice. No young fellow in the world at any point looked so gorgeous, as he naturally suspected he did, behind a fifteen penny stogie or a meerschaum!

These comments apply with ten times power to the utilization of inebriating drinks to make cash, requires a reasonable mind. A man must see that two and two make four; he should lay every one of his arrangements with reflection and planning, and intently analyze every one of the subtleties and the intricate details of business. As no man can prevail in business except if he has a mind to empower him to lay his arrangements, and motivation to direct him in their execution, thus, regardless of how plentifully a man might be honored with knowledge, in the event that the cerebrum is obfuscated, and his judgment distorted by inebriating drinks, it is beyond the realm of possibilities for him to effectively carry on business. The number of good open doors have passed, never to return, while a man was tasting a "social glass," with his companion! The number of silly deals that have been made under the impact of the nerving, which briefly makes its casualty think he is rich.

The number of significant possibilities that have been postponed until to-morrow, and afterward everlastingly, on the grounds that the wine cup has tossed the framework into a condition of stupor, killing the energies so crucial for outcome in business. Verily, wine is a faker. The utilization of inebriating drinks as a refreshment, is as much a captivation, just like the smoking of opium by the Chinese, and the previous is very as horrendous to the progress of the money manager as the last option. It is a ridiculous insidiousness, totally shaky in the illumination of reasoning; religion or excellent. It is the parent of practically every other malicious person in our country.

KEY ONE

TRY NOT TO MISSTEP YOUR LIVELIHOOD

The most well thought out plan, and the one generally certain of achievement for the young fellow beginning throughout everyday life, is to choose the occupation which is generally friendly as he would prefer.

Guardians and watchmen are in many cases too careless concerning this. It is very normal for a dad to say, for instance: "I have five young men.

I will make Billy a priest; John a legal counselor; Tom a specialist, and Dick a rancher." He then goes into town and looks to see how he will manage Sammy. He gets back and says "Sammy, I see watch-production is a decently cultured business; I figure I will make you a goldsmith." He does this, no matter what Sam's regular tendencies, or virtuoso.

We are all, no question, brought into the world for a shrewd reason. There is so a lot variety in our minds as in our faces. Some are conceived as regular mechanics, while having extraordinary repugnance for hardware.
Let twelve young men of a decade get together, and you will before long notice a few are "shaving" out some brilliant gadget; working with locks or convoluted apparatus. At the point when they were.

However, at five years of age, their dad could track down no toy to satisfy them like a riddle. They are regular mechanics; however the other eight or nine young men have various aptitudes. I have a place with the last option class; I never had the smallest love for a system; on the contrary, I have a kind of loathing for muddled hardware. I won't ever have creativity enough to shave a juice tap so it wouldn't spill. I never could make a pen that I could compose with, or figure out the guideline of a steam motor. In the event that a man was to accept such a kid as I was, and endeavor to make a watchmaker of him, the kid may, after an apprenticeship of five or seven years, have the option to dismantle What's more, set up a watch; yet all through life he would be stirring up slopes and holding onto each reason for leaving his work and sitting away his time. Watch making is frightful.

Except if a man enters upon the employment expected for him naturally, and the most appropriate to his unconventional virtuoso, he will fail. I'm happy to accept that a greater part of people really do track down their right work. However we see numerous who have mixed up their calling, from the smithy up (or down) to the pastor. You will see, for example, that phenomenal etymologist the "learned smithy," who should have been an educator of dialects; and you might have seen legal counselors, specialists and ministers who were better fitted naturally for the iron block or the lap stone.

KEY TWO
PERFECT SPOT, IDEAL OPPORTUNITY

In the wake of getting the right area, you should be mindful so as to choose the appropriate area. You might have been ready to deal with a lodging manager, and they say it requires a virtuoso to "know how to keep an inn." You

could lead an inn predictably, furthermore, give agreeably to 500 visitors consistently; yet, assuming you ought to find your home in a little town where there is no railroad correspondence or public travel, the area would be your ruin. You should don't initiate business where there are currently enough to fulfill all needs in a similar occupation.

KEY THREE
STAY AWAY FROM DEBT LIKE A PLAGUE

Young fellows beginning in life ought to try not to run into obligation. That is guaranteed. There is barely anything more that hauls an individual down like obligation. It is a survival situation to get sick, yet we track down numerous young fellows, barely out of his "teenagers, running in the red and indeed, this has been happening for a really long time as long as men and history could be recollected. He meets a pal and expresses,

"Check this: I have our trust for another suit of garments." He appears to view the garments as to such an extent given to him; indeed, it habitually is thus, at the same time, on the off chance that he prevails with regards to paying and, gets trusted once more, he is embracing a propensity which will keep him in destitution through life.

Obligation denies a man of his sense of pride, and makes him nearly detest himself Snorting and moaning and working for what he has eaten up or broken down, what's more, presently when he is called upon to settle up, he doesn't have anything to show for his cash;

This is appropriately named "working for a dead pony." I don't discuss vendors trading on layaway, or of the people who purchase using a credit card to turn the buy to a benefit. Cash is in certain regards like fire; it is an extremely phenomenal worker yet an awful expert. At the point when you make them ace you; when interest is continually stacking toward you, it will hold you down in the most exceedingly terrible sort of bondage. Yet, let cash work for you, and you have the most fired up worker on the planet. It is no eye-worker. There isn't anything quicken or lifeless that will work so steadfastly as cash when set at revenue, all around got. It works night and day, and in wet or dry climates. So don't allow it to neutralize you; assuming you do there is no way for outcome in life most definitely.

KEY FOUR

PERSEVERANCE IS ANOTHER WORD FOR CONFIDENCE

At the point when a man is in the correct way, he should drive forward. I talk about this on the grounds that there are a few people who are "conceived tired;" normally sluggish and having no confidence and no diligence. Yet, they can develop these characteristics.

It is this go on fixation, this assurance not to let the repulsions or the blues claim you, to cause you to loosen up your energies in the battle for freedom, which you should develop.

The number of have nearly arrived at the objective of their aspiration, at the same time, losing confidence in themselves, have loosened up their energies, and the brilliant award has been lost until the end of time.

It is, no question, frequent evident, as Shakespeare says:

There is a tide in the undertakings of men, which, taken at the flood, drives on to fortune. In the event that you falter, some bolder hand will loosen up before you and get the prize. Recall the adage of Solomon: He becometh unfortunate that dealeth with a leeway hand; however the hand of the persevering maketh rich.

Tirelessness is some of the time yet a different way to say confidence. Numerous people normally look on the clouded side of life, and take on pointless risk. They are conceived so. Then they request exhortation, and they will be administered by one breeze and unceremoniously passed up another, and can't depend upon themselves. Until you can get so you can depend upon yourself, you want not to anticipate succeeding.

Men who have met with financial turns around, and totally dedicated self-destruction, since they figured they would never defeat their mishap. Be that as it may, I have known other people who have met more serious monetary troubles, and have connected them over by straightforward diligence, supported by a firm conviction that they were doing legitimately, and that Provision would beat evil with great. You will see this represented in any circle of life.

KEY FIVE

ANYTHING YOU DO, DO IT WITH ALL YOUR STRENGTH

Work at it, if essential, early and late, in season and unavailable, not leaving a stone unturned, and never conceding for a solitary hour that which can be done similarly also now. The old adage is brimming with truth and signifying, "Whatever is worth doing by any means, merits getting along nicely." Numerous a man obtains a fortune by doing his business completely, while his neighbor stays poor forever, in light of the fact that he as it were half gets it done. Desire, energy, industry, tirelessness, are irreplaceable requirements for outcome in business. Fortune generally inclines toward the fearless, and never helps a man who doesn't help himself. It will not do to invest your energy like Mr. Mike, in hanging tight for something to "turn up." To such men one of two things ordinarily "turns up:" the poorhouse or the prison; for inaction breeds vices, and garments a man in clothes. The unfortunate prodigal drifter tells a rich man:

"I have found there is sufficient cash on the planet for us all, if it was similarly isolated; this should be finished, and we will be in every way content."

Yet, was the reaction, "in the event that everyone was like you, it would be spent in two months, and what might you do then, at that point? Gracious! Partition once more; continue to separate, obviously!

I was as of late perusing in a London paper a record of a like rational homeless person who was removed from a modest motel since he was unable to pay his bill, however he had a roll of papers standing out of his jacket pocket, which, upon assessment, ended up being his arrangement for taking care of the public obligation of Britain without the guide of a penny.

Individuals must do as Cromwell said: "trust in Provision, yet stay prepared." Do your piece of the work, or you will fail.

Mahomet, one evening, while at the same time staying in the desert, heard one of his exhausted devotees comment: "I will free my camel, and trust it to God!" "No, no, not really," said the prophet, "tie thy camel, and trust it to God!" Give your best for yourselves, and afterward trust to Provision, or karma, or anything that you please to call it, for the rest.

KEY SIX

RELY ON YOUR OWN EFFORT

**The eye of the business owner is many times
worth more than the hands of a dozen
workers.**

In the idea of things, a specialist can't be as
devoted to his manager as to himself. Numerous
businesses will bring to mind examples where

the best workers have disregarded significant focuses which could never have gotten away from their own perception as an owner. No man has a privilege to hope to prevail throughout everyday life except if he grasps his business, and it's not possible for anyone to figure out his business completely except if he learns it by private application and experience. A man might be a producer: he must gain proficiency with the many subtleties of his business actually; he will learn something consistently, and he will find he will make botches practically consistently. Also, these very botches are served to him in the method of encounters on the off chance that he yet notices them. He will resemble the Yankee tin-seller, who, having been cheated as to quality in the acquisition of his product, said: "All right, there's a little data to be acquired consistently; I won't ever be cheated in that way once more." In this way a man purchases his experience, and it is the best kind on the off chance that not bought at too dear a rate.

This is by all accounts an inconsistency in wording, however it isn't, Furthermore, there is extraordinary insight in the saying. It is, truth be told, a consolidated proclamation of what I have previously said. It is to say; "you should practice your wariness in laying your arrangements, yet be strong in doing them." A man who is everything alert, won't ever set out to grab hold and find true success; and a man who is all strength, is only wild, and must ultimately fall flat. A man might go on "'change" and make fifty, or 100,000 bucks by hypothesizing in stocks, at a solitary activity. However, assuming he has straightforward strength without alertness, it is a simple possibility, and what he gains today he will lose to-morrow. You should have both the watchfulness and the intensity, to guarantee a good outcome.

The Rothschild have another saying: "have nothing to do with an unfortunate man or spot." In other words, have nothing to do with a man or spot which never succeeds, on the grounds that, albeit a man might have all the earmarks of tell the truth and astute, yet assuming he attempts either thing and consistently fizzles, it is because of some shortcoming or ailment that you will most likely be unable to find yet by the by which should exist.

There is nothing of the sort on the planet as karma. There never was a man who could go out in the first part of the day and find a satchel brimming with gold in the road to-day, furthermore, one more to-morrow, a large number of days: He might do so once in his life; In any case, most definitely, he is as obligated to lose it as to track it down. Like causes produce outcomes. On the off chance that a man embraces the legitimate techniques to find lasting success, "karma" won't forestall him. On the off chance that he doesn't succeed, there are explanations behind it, albeit, maybe, he will be unable to see them.

KEY SEVEN

UTILIZE THE BEST DEVICE

Men in drawing in workers ought to be mindful so as to get the best. Comprehend, you can't have too great apparatuses to work with, and there is no instrument you ought to be as specific as, probably as living instruments. On the off chance that you get a decent one, keeping him is better, then continue to change. He gets the hang of something consistently; and you circular segment benefited by the experience he gets. He is worth more to you this year than last, and he is the last man to leave behind, given his propensities are great, and he proceeds with devotion. In the event that, as he gets more important, he requests an over the top increment of compensation; on the assumption that you can't manage without him, let him go. When and if at any time you have such a worker, consistently release him; first, to persuade him that his place might be provided, and second, since he is useless assuming he assumes he is significant and can't be saved.

Be that as it may, you would keep him, if conceivable, to benefit from the aftereffect of his experience. A significant component in a representative is the cerebrum. You can see bills up, hands needed, however "hands" are not worth an extraordinary arrangement without "heads." Those men who possess brainpower and experience are thus the most significant and not to be promptly left behind; it is better for them, as well as yourself, to keep them, at sensible advances in their compensations now and again.

KEY EIGHT

DO NOT GROW ABOVE YOUR BUSINESS

Young fellows after they traverse their business preparing, or apprenticeship, rather than seeking after their hobby and ascending in their business, will frequently lie about sitting idle. They say; "I have taken in my business, yet I won't be an employee; what is the object of learning my exchange or calling, except if I lay down a good foundation for myself?

Do you have cash-flow to begin with?

No, yet I will have it.

How are you going to get it?

I will tell you secretly; I have a rich old auntie, and she will pass on pretty soon; however in the event that she doesn't, I hope to discover some rich elderly person who will loan me two or three thousand to give me a beginning.

Assuming that I just get the means to begin with, I will get along admirably.

There could be no more prominent error than when a young fellow accepts he will prevail with acquired cash. What's more, observe that this sort of discussion is as yet rehashed even into the

21st 100 years. Why? Since each man's experience matches with that of Mr. Astor, who said, "it was more challenging for him to aggregate his initial thousand bucks, than every one of the succeeding millions that made up his epic fortune." Cash is a deadbeat except if you know its worth by experience. Give a kid twenty thousand bucks and put him in business, and the odds are good that he will lose each dollar of it before he is a year more established. Like purchasing a ticket in the lottery and drawing an award, it is "what is easy to get is never really appreciated." He doesn't have the foggiest idea about the worth of it; nothing merits anything, except if it costs exertion. Without abstemiousness and economy; tolerance and constancy, and beginning with capital which you have not procured, you don't know how to prevail with regards to aggregating. Young fellows, rather than "hanging tight for dead men's shoes," ought to be up and doing, for there is no class of people who are so unaccommodating as to biting the dust as these rich old individuals, and it is lucky for the hopeful beneficiaries that it is so. The vast majority of the rich men of our nation today, began in life as poor young men, with decided wills, industry, constancy, economy and great propensities. They continued bit by bit, bringing in their own cash and saving it; and this is the most ideal way to get a fortune. Stephen Girard began life as an unfortunate lodge kid. What's more, I kicked the bucket worth 9,000,000 bucks. A.T. Stewart was an unfortunate Irish kid; and he paid charges on a million and a half dollars of pay, each year. John Jacob Astor was an unfortunate rancher kid, and passed on worth twenty millions. Cornelius Vanderbilt started life paddling a boat from Staten Island to New York; he introduced our government with a steamship worth 1,000,000 of dollars, and kicked the bucket worth fifty million. "There is no regal street to learning," says the precept, and I might say it is similarly evident, "there is no regal street to riches." Yet I think there is a regal street to both. The street to learning is an illustrious one; the street that empowers the understudy to grow his keenness and add consistently to his load of information, until, in the charming course of scholarly development, he can settle the most significant issues, to count the stars, to break down each iota of the globe, and to quantify the atmosphere is a lofty interstate, and it is the main street worth voyaging.

So concerning abundance: happen in certainty, concentrate on the principles, or more all things, concentrate on human instinct; for "the appropriate investigation of humankind is man," and you will find that while growing the mind and the muscles, your extended experience will empower you consistently to collect increasingly more principal, which will increase itself by interest and otherwise, until you arrive at a state of independence. You will find, as a general thing that the poor boys get rich and the rich boys get poor.

For instance, a rich man, at his death, leaves a large estate to his family. His eldest sons, who have helped him earn his fortune, known by experience the value of money; and they take their inheritance and add to it. The separate portions of the young children are placed at interest, and the little fellows are patted on the head, and told a dozen times a day, "you are rich; you will never have to work, you can always have whatever you wish, for you were born with a golden spoon in your mouth." The young heir soon finds out what that means; he has the finest dresses and playthings; he is crammed with sugar candies and almost "killed with kindness," and he passes from school to school, petted and flattered. He becomes arrogant and self-conceited, abuses his teachers, and carries everything with a high hand. He knows nothing of the real value of money, having never earned any; but he knows all about the "golden spoon" business. At college, he invites his poor fellow-students to his room, where he "wines and dines" them. He is cajoled and caressed, and called a glorious good follower, because he is so lavish with his money. He gives his game suppers, drives his fast horses, invites his chums to fetes and parties, determined to have lots of "good times." He spends the night in frolics and debauchery, and leads off his companions with the familiar song, "we won't go home till morning." He gets them to join him in pulling down signs, taking gates from their hinges and throwing them into backyards and horse-ponds. If the police arrest them, he knocks them down, is taken to the lockup, and joyfully foots the bills. Ah! My boys," he cries, what is the use of being rich, if you can't enjoy yourself? He might more truly say, if you can't make a fool of yourself; but he is fast, hates slow things, and doesn't see it. Young men loaded down with other people's money are almost sure to lose all they inherit, and they acquire all sorts of bad habits which, in the majority of cases, ruin them in health, purse and character. In this country, one generation follows another, and the poor of today are rich in the next generation, or the third. Their experience leads them on, and they become rich, and they leave vast riches to their young children. These children, having been reared in luxury, are inexperienced and get poor; and after long experience another generation comes on and gathers up riches again in turn. And thus history repeats itself, and happy is he who by listening to the experience of others avoids the rocks and shoals on which so many have been wrecked.

In this Republican country, the man makes the business. No matter whether he is a blacksmith, a shoemaker, a farmer, banker or lawyer, so long as his business is legitimate, he may be a gentleman. So any "legitimate" business is a double blessing: it helps the man engaged in it, and also helps others. The Farmer supports his own family, but he also benefits the merchant or mechanic who needs the products of his farm. The tailor not only makes a living by his trade, but he also benefits the farmer, the clergyman and others who cannot make their own clothing. But all these classes often may be gentlemen.

The great ambition should be to excel all others engaged in the same occupation. The college-student who was about to graduate said to an old lawyer: I have not yet decided which profession I will follow. Is your profession full?

The basement is much crowded, but there is plenty of room up-stairs, was the witty and truthful reply.

No profession, trade, or calling, is overcrowded in the upper story.

Wherever you find the most honest and intelligent merchant or banker, or the best lawyer, the best doctor, the best clergyman, the best shoemaker, carpenter, or anything else, that man is most sought for, and has always enough to do. As a nation, Americans are too superficial they are striving to get rich quickly, and do not generally do their business as substantially and thoroughly as they should, but whoever excels all others in his own line, if his habits are good and his integrity undoubted, cannot fail to secure abundant patronage, and the wealth that naturally follows. Let your motto then always be "Excelsior," for by living up to it there is no such word as fail.

KEY NINE

LEARN SOMETHING USEFUL

Every man should make his son or daughter learn some useful trade or profession, so that in these days of changing fortunes of being rich today and poor tomorrow they may have something tangible to fall back upon. This provision might save many persons from misery, who by some unexpected turn of fortune have lost all their means.

KEY TEN

LET HOPE PREDOMINATE, BUT BE NOT TOO VISIONARY

Many people are always kept poor, because they are too visionary. Every project looks to them like a certain success, and therefore they keep changing from one business to another, always in hot water, always "under the harrow. The plan of "counting the chickens before they are hatched" is an ancient date, but it does not seem to improve by age.

KEY ELEVEN

DO NOT SCATTER YOUR POWERS

Engage in one kind of business only, and stick to it faithfully until you succeed, or until your experience shows that you should abandon it. A constant hammering on one nail will generally drive it home at last, so that it can be clinched. When a man's undivided attention is centered on one object, his mind will constantly be suggesting improvements of value, which would escape him if his brain was occupied by a dozen different subjects at once. Many fortunes have slipped through a man's fingers because he was engaged in too many occupations at a time. There is good sense in the old caution against having too many irons in the fire at once.

KEY TWELVE

BE   **SYSTEMATIC**

Men should be systematic in their business. A person who does business by rule, having a time and place for everything, doing his work promptly, will accomplish twice as much and with half the trouble of those who do it carelessly and slipshod. By introducing system into all your transactions, doing one thing at a time, always meeting appointments with punctuality, you find leisure for pastime and recreation; whereas the man who only half does one thing, and then turns to something else, and half does that, will have his business at loose ends, and will never know when his day's work is done, for it never will be done. Of course, there is a limit to all these rules. We must try to preserve the happy medium, for there is such a thing as being too systematic. There are men and women, for instance, who put away things so carefully that they can never find them again.

KEY THIRTEEN

READ THE PAPERS DAILY

Always take a trustworthy newspaper, and thus keep thoroughly posted in regard to the transactions of the world. He who is without a newspaper is cut off from his species. In these days of the Web, numerous significant creations and upgrades in each part of exchange are being made, and he who don't counsel the papers will before long find himself and his business abandoned.

KEY FOURTEEN

BE CAREFUL WITH OUTDOOR ACTIVITY

We at times see men who have gotten fortunes, abruptly become poor. Much of the time, this emerges from excessiveness, and frequently from gaming, and other unfortunate behavior patterns. As often as possible it happens in light of the fact that a man has been participating in outside tasks, or the like. At the point when he gets wealthy in his authentic business, he is told a fantastic theory where he can make a score of thousands. He is continually complimented by his companions, who let him know that he is conceived fortunate, that all that he contacts transforms into gold. Presently assuming he fails to remember that his conservative tendencies, his integrity of directness and an individual thoughtfulness regarding a business which he perceived, caused his progress throughout everyday life, he will pay attention to the alarm voices.

A couple of days pass and it is found he should place in 10,000 bucks more: not long after he is told "it is good," however certain issues not anticipated, require a development of 20,000 bucks more, which will present to him a rich collect; however before the opportunity arrives around to understand, the air pocket explodes, he loses all he is equipped with, and afterward he realizes what he should have known at the first, that despite how effective a man might be in his own business, that's what assuming that he abandons what's more, connects a sick business which he doesn't have any idea of, he is like Samson when shorn of his locks his solidarity has left, and he becomes like different men. In the event that a man has a lot of cash, he should put something in all things that seems to guarantee a positive outcome, and that will presumably help humankind; yet let the totals hence put be moderate in sum, and never let a man stupidly imperil a fortune that he has procured a real way, by financial planning it things which he has had no insight.

KEY FIFTEEN

TRY NOT TO INDORSE WITHOUT SECURITY

No man should ever endorse a note or become security, for any man, be it his dad or sibling, to a more prominent degree than he can stand to lose and mind nothing about, without taking great security. Here is a man that is worth twenty thousand bucks; he is doing a flourishing assembling or commercial exchange; you are resigned and living on your cash; he comes to you and say you know that I am valued at 10,000 bucks, and don't owe a dollar; on the off chance that I had 2,500 bucks in real money, I could buy a specific parcel of merchandise and twofold my cash in several months; will you indorse my note for that sum?

You mirror that he is valued at 10,000 bucks, and you bring about no gamble by underwriting his note; you like to oblige him, and you loan your name without avoiding potential risk of getting security. Soon after, he shows you the note with your underwriting dropped, and tells you, presumably genuinely, that he created the gain that he anticipated by the activity," you mirror that you have done a decent activity, and the idea encourages you. Before long, exactly the same thing happens once more and you rehash it; you have proactively fixed the impression in your mind that endorsing his notes without security is completely protected.

In any case, the difficulty is, this man is getting cash too without any problem. He has just to take your note to the bank, get it limited and take the money. He gets cash for the time being without exertion; without burden to himself. Presently mark the result. He sees an opportunity for hypotheses beyond his business. An impermanent venture of just $15,000 is required. It makes certain to return before a note at the bank would be expected. He puts a note for that sum before you. You sign it precisely. Being immovably persuaded that your companion is dependable and reliable; you endorse his notes as an expected result. Tragically the hypothesis doesn't reach a critical stage as soon as was normal, and one more $15,000 note should be limited to take up the last one when due. Before this note develops the hypothesis has demonstrated an utter disappointment and all the cash is lost. Does the washout tell his companion, the endorser, that he has lost a portion of his fortune? Not in any way shape or form. He doesn't for a moment even notice that he has estimated by any stretch of the imagination. In any case, he has energized; the soul of hypothesis has held onto him; he sees others making huge totals along these lines we rarely know about the failures, and, like different theorists, he "searches for his cash where he loses it." He attempts once more, underwriting notes has become constant with you, and at each misfortune he gets your signature for however much he needs. At long last you find your companion has lost the entirety of his property and all of yours. You are overpowered with shock and sorrow, and you say "it is something hard; my companion here has demolished me," be that as it may, you ought to add, "I have likewise demolished him. Assuming you had said in any case, "I will oblige you, however I never indorse without taking more than adequate security," he could not have gone past the length of his tie, and he couldn't have ever been enticed away from his real business. It is an

Exceptionally perilous thing, in this manner, to allow individuals to get ownership of cash too effectively; it entices them to perilous hypotheses, if that's it. So with the young fellow beginning in business; let him figure out the worth of cash by procuring it. At the point when he comprehends its worth, then oil the wheels a little in assisting him with beginning business, yet recall, men who get cash with too extraordinary office can't normally succeed. You should get the first dollars by difficult times, and at some penance, to see the value in the worth of those dollars.

KEY SIXTEEN

PUBLICIZE YOUR BUSINESS

We as a whole depend, pretty much, upon the general population for our help. We as a whole exchange with general society legal counselors, specialists, shoemakers, craftsmen, metalworkers, actors, show stagers, railroad presidents, and school teachers. The people who manage the public should be cautious that their products are important; that they are authentic, furthermore, will give fulfillment. At the point when you get an article which you know is going to satisfy your clients, and that when they have attempted it, they will feel they have made out really well, then spread the word that you have it. Be cautious to promote it in some shape or other in light of the fact that it is clear that if a man has very great an article available to be purchased, and no one knows it, it will present to him no return.

Where almost everyone pursues, and where papers are given and circled in releases of 5,000 to 200,000, it would be very imprudent in the event that this channel was not exploited to arrive at people in general in promoting. A paper goes into the family, and is perused by spouse and youngsters, as well as the top of the home; subsequently hundreds and thousands of individuals may peruse your notice, while you are taking care of your standard business. Many, maybe, read it while you are sleeping. The entire way of thinking of life is, first "sow," then "harvest." That is the manner in which the rancher does; he establishes his potatoes and corn, and plants his grain, and afterward approaches something different, and the opportunity arrives when he procures. Yet, he never procures first and sows a while later. This guideline applies to all sorts of business, and to nothing more prominently than to publicizing. If a man has a veritable article, it is basically impossible that in which he can harvest all the more favorably than by "planting" to general society along these lines. He should, obviously, have a great article, and one which will satisfy his clients; anything misleading will not succeed forever in light of the fact that general society is more astute than many envision. Men and ladies are narrow minded, and we as a whole incline toward buying where we can maximize our cash and we attempt to find out where we can most clearly do as such. You might publicize a deceptive article, and initiate many individuals to call and get it once, yet they will condemn you as a faker and deceiver, and your business will progressively cease to exist and leave you poor. This is correct. Hardly any individuals can securely rely on possibility custom. All of you really want to have your clients return furthermore, buy once more.

So a man who promotes at all should keep it up until the public knows who furthermore, what he is, and what his business is, or, more than likely the cash put resources into publicizing is lost.

A few men have a curious virtuoso for composing a striking promotion, one that will capture the consideration of the peruses right away. This reality, obviously, gives the public an incredible benefit. In some cases a man makes

himself well known by an extraordinary sign or
an inquisitive presentation in his window.

KEY SEVENTEEN
BE CONSIDERATE AND KIND TO YOUR CLIENTS

Courteousness and politeness are the best capital at any point to put resources into business. Enormous stores, overlaid signs, blazing commercials, will all demonstrate unavailing in the event that you or your workers treat your benefactors suddenly. Actually, the more kind and liberal a man is, the more liberal will be the support given upon him. Like generates like. The one who gives the best measure of merchandise of a related quality for the least total actually saving for himself a benefit will for the most part succeed best over the long haul. This carries us to the brilliant rule, "As ye ought that men to do to you, do ye likewise to them" and they will improve by you than if you generally regarded them as though you needed to get the most you could out of them for the least return. Men who drive sharp deals with their clients, going about as though they never expected to see them once

more, won't be mixed up. They won't ever see
them from now onward as clients.

KEY EIGHTEEN

BE MAGNANIMOUS

Obviously men ought to be magnanimous, on the grounds that it is an obligation and a joy. In any case, even as an issue of strategy, on the off chance that you have no higher impetus, you will find that the liberal man will order support, while the sordid, uncharitable penny pincher will be kept away from.

Solomon says: "There is that scattereth but increaseth; and there is that withholdeth more than meet, yet it tendeth to destitution." obviously the as it were genuine cause is what is from the heart.

The most ideal sort of cause is to help the individuals who will help themselves. Unbridled almsgiving, without inquisitiveness into the value of the candidate, is terrible in each sense. In any case, to look out and discreetly help the people who are battling for themselves purposes, is the sort that dissipates but increments. Yet, don't fall into the thought that a few people practice giving a request rather than a potato, and a blessing rather than bread, to the hungry. It is simpler to make Christians with full stomachs than void.

KEY NINETEEN

TRY NOT TO BLAB

A few men have a silly propensity for revealing their business mysteries. On the off chance that they bring in cash they like to let their neighbors know about the way things were finished. Nothing is acquired by this, and periodically much is lost. Don't express anything about your benefits, your expectations, your assumptions, your aims. Furthermore, this ought to apply to letters as well as to discussion.

Financial specialists should compose letters, however they ought to be cautious what they put in them. On the off chance that you are losing cash, be particularly careful and not recount it, or you will lose you're standing.

KEY TWEWNTY

PROTECT YOUR HONESTY

Respectability is more valuable than precious stones or rubies. This exhortation was frightfully fiendish, yet it was the actual pith of idiocy: It was as much as to say in the event that you find it challenging to get cash genuinely, you can undoubtedly get it untrustworthy. Not to realize that the most troublesome thing in life is to bring in cash untrustworthiness.

Not to realize that our penitentiaries are brimming with men who endeavored to follow this exhortation; not to comprehend that no man can be deceptive, without before long being found out, and that when his absence of rule is found, essentially every road to progress is shut against him until the end of time. The general population appropriately avoids all whose respectability is questioned. Regardless of how well-mannered and lovely and obliging a man might be, not a solitary one of us set out to manage him on the off chance that we suspect "bogus loads and measures. Severe trustworthiness, not just lies at the groundwork of all outcomes throughout everyday life monetarily, yet in each and every other regard. Solid respectability of character is significant. It gets to its owner a harmony and satisfaction which can't be accomplished without it which no sum of cash, or houses and grounds can buy. A man who is known to stringently be genuine, might be very poor, however he has the satchels of all the local area at his removal for all know that assuming he vows to return what he acquires, he will never frustrate them. As a simple matter of self-centeredness, thus, in the event that a man had no higher thought process in telling the truth, all will track down that the adage can never neglect to be valid, that genuineness is the smartest strategy.

To get rich isn't generally comparable to finding actual success. "There are numerous rich unfortunate men," while there are numerous others, fair and dedicated men also, ladies, who have never had such a lot of cash as a few rich people waste in seven days, however who are by and by truly more extravagant and more joyful than any man can at any point be while he is a violator of the greater laws of his being. The over the top love of cash, almost certainly, might be and is "the foundation of all malicious, however, cash itself, when appropriately utilized, isn't just a helpful thing to have in the house," however manages the cost of the delight of gift our race by empowering its holder to expand the extent of human satisfaction and human impact. The longing for abundance is almost all inclusive, and none can say it isn't commendable, given the holder of it acknowledges its liabilities, and utilizes it as a companion to mankind.

The historical backdrop of getting riches, which is business, is a background marked by civilization, and any place exchange has thrived most, there, as well, have craftsmanship and science delivered the noblest natural products. As something overall, cash getters are, truth be told the sponsors of our race. To them, in an extraordinary measure, are we obliged for our establishments of learning and of craftsmanship, our foundations, universities and houses of worship? It is no contention against the craving for, or the ownership of riches, to express that there are in some cases misanthropes who crowd cash just for accumulating and who have no higher desire than to get a handle on all that which draws near their compass. As we have once in a while frauds in religion, and revolutionaries in legislative issues, so there are sporadically grumpy persons among cash getters. These, notwithstanding, are as it were exemptions for the overall guideline. Yet, when, in this country, we track down such an irritation what's more, hindrance as a penny pincher, we recall with appreciation that in America we have no laws of primogeniture, and that in the proper method of nature the time will come when the stored residue will be dispersed to support humanity. To all people: bring in cash sincerely, and not in any case, for Shakespeare has genuinely said, he that needs cash, means, and content, is without three old buddies.

KEY TWENTY ONE
CHOOSE AND MAKE DECISIONS CAREFULLY

Every decision has a cost, so be sure to consider your options too often, people make financial decisions without thinking through the consequences. For example, a consumer feels they must have a product, doesn't have enough cash, and uses a credit card to make the purchase without thinking about how much it will cost to pay off the debt. Or a couple buys a house without fully understanding the terms of the mortgage loan. When you choose between two things, you automatically give something up. A decision to buy an expensive car is a decision not to use that money to buy other goods or services, or make an additional payment on your mortgage, or put extra money in your children's college savings fund. Before making that impulse purchase, be sure to think about the cost of your choices.

CONCLUSION

Taking everything into account, "The Wealth Compass: 21 Keys to unlocking financial success" offers significant bits of knowledge and direction for those looking to make monetary progress. Through its complete methodology, the book investigates eighteen fundamental keys that can make ready for monetary overflow. From understanding the influence of attitude and objective setting to executing successful growing long term financial stability methodologies, this book outfits pursers with the information and instruments expected to explore the domain of individual accounting. By following the standards illustrated in "The Wealth Compass, pursuers can possibly change their monetary direction and make an existence of flourishing and overflow. It is a must for anybody seeking to open their monetary potential and create enduring financial stability.